Uga

Hunkers Down in Athens Town

Jack Weaver

Illustrated by Glenda Brown Ingram

Published

By

Weaver Jack Company
P.O. Box 4263
Canton, Georgia 30114

ISBN: 0-9773370-0-6
Library of Congress Control Number: 2005908646

Page layout and cover design by Timothy W. Beasley

Printed in Hong Kong

PREFACE

Anyone who has ever attended a college football game in the South can tell you that there is no experience quite like it. The game itself is enhanced by the many traditions which are unique for each institution. In this book, the University of Georgia mascot, Uga, tells the story of a typical football weekend in Athens, Georgia. Follow his story from the time he leaves his home in Savannah, to his descriptions of Georgia traditions, and finally the depiction of the game itself. This book is sure to captivate the interest of all future members of the "Bulldawg Nation" and is the first volume of the children's book series, "College Mascots Tell the Story of a Traditional Football Weekend on Campus."

ABOUT THE AUTHOR

Jack Weaver has spent over 30 years educating youth in Georgia's Cherokee County School System, where he has served as a teacher and principal. He holds three degrees from the University of Georgia; thus it is only natural that he would combine his love for teaching reading to young people with his fondness for the institution where he received much of his higher education. As an avid college football fan, he hopes that this book will instill a desire for children to read and continue to support special traditions that have been passed down to football fans of the University of Georgia, making each of them "proud to be a Georgia Bulldawg!"

ABOUT THE ILLUSTRATOR

Glenda Brown Ingram is a native Georgian and a self-taught artist who loves to draw and paint. Her talents in the art field were first recognized as a muralist as many of her works can be found adorning the walls of schools in North Georgia. Mrs. Ingram attended college where she completed courses in the field of education. Her husband, Rick, is a 1979 UGA alumnus and her son, Evan, is a future bulldog and the inspiration for his mother's work. When she is not "doodling," as she likes to describe it, Mrs. Ingram enjoys spending her spare time "antiquing."

Dedicated to the following:

Former and present educators of the Cherokee County (Georgia) School System, who assisted me in acquiring a quality education, and also, those individuals who have served as co-workers for a career spanning over 30 years.

Educators of my alma maters Kennesaw State University and the University of Georgia, especially Dr. Ronald Simpson (UGA) who has served as a true professional educator, advisor, mentor, and friend.

Vernie N. Weaver and Florence Ruthell (Cline) Weaver, whose Christian influences as parents have instilled a desire for me to pursue good values in respect for the personal sacrifices which they made to assist me in acquiring my education.

Carolyn (Thomason) Weaver, whose unyielding support as my wife of 26 years has been invaluable as a partner in the pursuit of all endeavors.

All future members of the "Bulldawg Nation," with hopes that the wonderful traditions of UGA football will continue for the enjoyment of generations to come.

Although the football game isn't until tomorrow, I can already imagine hearing the stadium announcer say, "It's time to tee it up between the hedges." Just a few more things to pack in my bag and I will be ready to leave for Athens town. Whoops, I can't forget to put in my red sweater with the black Georgia "G," or the fans would never forgive me. Finally, my owner readies me for the trip by brushing my fur one last time, and after a quick walk, we are then ready to roll. It will now only be a matter of hours until I will be inside the huge stadium for the big game.

As we leave the moss draped trees of South Georgia behind, the music of "Glory, Glory to Old Georgia" blares in my ears over the car speakers. After about three hours of listening to "Hail to Georgia" and chants of the Redcoat Band, I feel as pumped as a dog could feel as we pull into the Classic City of Athens. It is called that because it was named after the much older Athens, Greece, another city of beautifully styled homes and buildings where there is much love for the arts.

When the car finally comes to a stop on the University of Georgia campus, I am really ready to stretch my legs. I begin my walk on North Campus, which has always been one of my favorite areas to view the beautiful old buildings and do some people watching. This university is the oldest state chartered university in the nation as it was founded in 1785. I almost make the dreadful mistake of passing under the large iron arch instead of around it. The arch is patterned after the State of Georgia seal and has become known as the main entrance and symbol of the University of Georgia.

It has been said that if you walk under the arch before ever graduating from UGA, you will have very bad luck. Needless to say, I do not want this for me or the UGA football team, since I am their official mascot. I will take the longer path around the outside rather than passing directly under it.

Look! Over there is the Chapel, with the bell tower in back.

Most fans from opposing teams do not realize that the bell is rung by Bulldog fans until midnight after a game victory, and all night after a win over Georgia Tech. I certainly have heard a lot of clanging through the years as it is beautiful music to this English bulldog's ears.

Continuing back to my room located on the southern part of the campus, I pass in front of Sanford Stadium, the huge structure which surrounds the field where the football game will be played tomorrow. I pause for a moment to experience the silence which is almost haunting as I recall in my memory the deafening noise which has been created during many important games of the past. The neatly painted "Georgia G," along with the well trimmed hedges, gives the field almost the appearance of a garden. What a beautiful place! There surely isn't a setting more perfect for a college football game than on the manicured grass "between the hedges."

I could stand here on the bridge forever, but proceed I must, and across it I
go as I begin climbing Ag Hill.

"Ag" is short for agriculture as this is the area of the campus which has classes to prepare students for jobs in the agriculture sciences. My vet even went to school here.

Having continued my stroll through the tremendous college campus, I could have sworn that I heard some barking as I enter the Georgia Center and take the elevator up to my room. The sound certainly did not seem to be coming from one of my canine friends. Oh well, I could have just imagined it, or did I? After grabbing a bite to eat and then later exercising my jaws on a few ham bones, I am feeling really beat. I soon turn in for the night as I know the cheerleaders will be coming to get me early in the morning for the pep rallies, and I want to be at my best.

After a somewhat restful evening and a meaty breakfast, it's off to selected areas of the campus to get all the dog fans fired up with a few Georgia cheers. "Go dogs, sic' em" seems to be a favorite one and is repeated so often that it keeps ringing in my ears several minutes later.

I have to watch myself as I sometimes give an automatic lunge as I imagine hearing what sounds to me like a command. Although I like attention, I sure want to be careful not to turn too many heads for the wrong reason.

As the cars, trucks, and motor homes keep rolling into Athens, I don't believe I have ever seen so many red and black flags. Bulldog magnets adorn almost every vehicle. Some of the car horns are even programmed to play the first eight notes of "Glory, Glory to Old Georgia."

I am beginning to feel my stomach gnaw as tailgaters are setting up their tents and unpacking food for a pre-game picnic. Is that fried chicken I smell? After all, we are playing the Gamecocks today. Oh well, back to my room, where my owner has another menu planned for me prior to the famous "dog walk."

After eating a less desirable, but nutritious, canned meal, I'm ready to head to the stadium for the game. As I scuttle from the car onto Lumpkin Street, I cannot believe the huge crowd of people that has gathered, all wearing red and black clothes.

A narrow path exists through which the players and I begin to make our way closer to the stadium entrance. Was that a super hero I saw over in one side of the crowd? It sure looked like someone in a cape to me. Reckon how those fellows got bulldogs painted on the tops of their heads? Carnival face painting is nothing compared to this! As we continue down the small opening among wall to wall people, the sound almost becomes a constant roar as we enter a red and black funnel created by members of the Redcoat Band.

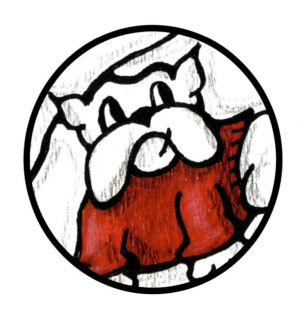

Upon passing through the main gate of the stadium, I have to briefly stop by an area which is decorated with fresh flowers. Tears drop from my eyes as I reflect on the service of other Ugas who are no longer living and whose remains are kept here in tombs. Can I ever live up to the high standards of sportsmanship which they have set for me?

Soon, I pass to the locker room and am really beginning to feel the heat of day. Or is it my blood pressure rising? I remind myself that it will be even hotter when well over 92,000 people get inside the stadium. I sure hope that someone thought to place a lot of ice over beside my dog house as my sagging tongue indicates the need for a major cool-down soon.

Although finding things more comfortable in the tunneled area beneath the stadium, the minutes pass slowly in anticipation. Finally, I notice echoes of "Georgia," then "Bulldogs" repeatedly coming from inside the stadium. The arena foundation almost seems to be vibrating from the sound. Suddenly, I hear the Redcoat Band strike up in the distance with a fanfare, and before I know it, the cheerleaders and I are leading the football players through a banner onto the field.

Chills go up and down my spine as a sea of red pom-poms suddenly erupt, bobbing back and forth all over the stadium. I spot a banner hanging just past the east end zone which says "Dawg Pound," but I'm certain that no dog pound has ever experienced the barking level which I hear now. Will my ears ever recover?

As I catch a quick breath, I get equipped for one of my favorite sideline duties. The cheerleaders are strapping a small camera to my head so all the fans can see views projected on a large screen of exactly what I am seeing. I hope they find this as exciting as I do.

Man, did you see our defender put a jolt on that player? With plays like that, it is no wonder why we are called the "junkyard dogs." After about two more plays, we receive the punt and are now on offense. Oh, there goes one of our players out to receive a long pass. Someone blocked my view, but I just heard the stadium announcer yell, "Touchdown, Georgia!" Or at least I believe that's what he hollered as the roar is now at a fever pitch. The band just struck up with "Glory, Glory to Old Georgia." Now, with the extra point good, they change tunes into "Hail to Georgia." College football, don't you love it? I just spotted Bulldog Network Announcer, Larry Munson, up in the broadcast booth. I wonder if he got so excited with the play that he broke his chair as he has been known to do in the past.

I'm so caught up in the action myself that the big fire hydrant over beside me is looking better each second. About this time, I hear a fan holler, "Hunker down, you hairy dogs!" Was she giving specific direction to me?

The excitement continues with our football dogs having their day until it seems all energy is drained from my body. The final straw came minutes earlier when the player from the opposing team got a little too close to our sideline and I snapped at him without really thinking. Ever since the Auburn game of a few seasons ago, I find myself jumping at opportunities to actively participate as they become available.

Finally, I hear the stadium announcer say, "Final score, Georgia 24, South Carolina 7. Be here next week when the Bulldogs take on the Tigers." Now as I am leashed, my owner leads me off the field as I struggle to stay on my feet. It often seems that he wants to go in one direction, and I want to go in another. Let the band play in the stands and the tailgate picnics begin. It's Saturday night in Athens!

Later, after visiting with friends around campus, I rest a little up in my room. While being still too charged up to sleep, it sure is nice listening to all the replays on the radio and watching the highlights of the game on television. I wonder where we will be in the national college football rankings when they are posted next week.

All too soon, the time comes to depart for home. Although glad that a mission has been accomplished, I am somewhat sad that this joyous event is over – at least for now. I had looked forward to this happening for a long time. Yes, it is all over, but suddenly my thoughts begin to turn to next weekend, when we will do all this once again. As I gaze through the rear windshield of the car and watch the red old hills of northeast Georgia fade into the distance, I can hardly wait for the game as I know there will be new adventures and more stories to be told. I've been told that it's not good to wish away days of your life, but I sure do wish it were next Saturday.

It's great to be a **Georgia Bulldog!**
Woof! Woof!